DATE DUE			

Incredible Facts about the Ocean

The Land Below, the Life Within
(Volume 2)

W. Wright Robinson

DILLON PRESS, INC.
Minneapolis, Minnesota 55415

Volumes 1 and 2 of Incredible Facts About the Ocean are dedicated to all children, with the hope that these future leaders will learn to understand, appreciate, and respect our beautiful and fascinating ocean world.

Library of Congress Cataloging in Publication Data
(Revised for volume 2)

Robinson, W. Wright.
    Incredible facts about the ocean.
    (Ocean world library)
    Includes bibliographies and indexes.
    Contents: [1] The restless blue salt water [2] The land below, the life within.
    1. Oceanography—Juvenile literature. 2. Oceanography. 3. Questions and answers. I. Title. II. Series.
GC21.5.R63   1987   551.46   85-25430
ISBN 0-87518-317-4 (v. 1)
ISBN 0-87518-358-1 (v. 2)

Dillon Press, Inc., 242 Portland Avenue South
Minneapolis, Minnesota 55415

Printed in the United States of America
        3 4 5 6 7 8 9 10 96 95 94 93 92 91 90

Contents

Acknowledgments

I would first like to thank Ms. Uva Dillon, publisher, for giving me the opportunity to publish two books on a topic that is very dear to me. The staff at Dillon Press also deserves a sincere "thank you." It is their professionalism and high standards that make both volumes of Incredible Facts About the Ocean everything I want them to be.

I wish to thank Dr. D. M. Dauer, Department of Biology, Old Dominion University; Dr. Gerald Johnson, Department of Geology, College of William and Mary; Dr. John Musick, Department of Ichthyology, Virginia Institute of Marine Science; and Ms. Clark Merriam, The Cousteau Society, Norfolk office, for their comments and suggestions after reviewing the manuscript for accuracy.

 *Ocean Facts*

Ocean Facts				
Ocean Name	Surface Area (mi²)*	Volume (mi³)*	Average Depth (ft)	Deepest Point (ft)
Pacific	63,690,000	161,090,000	13,355	36,200
Atlantic	37,828,000	86,687,000	12,100	29,000
Indian	25,283,000	48,030,000	10,037	25,344
Antarctic	12,352,000	28,633,000	12,240	21,038
Arctic	5,687,000	4,257,000	3,952	17,880
Total	144,840,000	328,697,000		

*"mi²" stands for square miles and "mi³" for cubic miles

 *Introduction*

Incredible Facts about the Ocean: The Floor Below, The Life Within answers many questions that are often asked about the land and the life in our oceans. Since more than 70 percent of the earth's surface is covered by water, people need to understand the beautiful and fascinating ocean world.

In this book you will discover how the oceans form deltas, islands, and sandbars and how the shape of land above sea level creates bodies of water such as seas, bays, gulfs, straits, and lagoons. You will also learn what the land beneath this huge world of water looks like. In addition, this book describes many interesting facts about some of the plants and animals that make the oceans their homes.

Incredible Facts about the Ocean can be used as a quick, easy reference source. Each chapter introduces a different topic; however, it is not necessary to read the entire chapter. Instead you can read the answer to any question that is of interest to you. Sometimes simple experiments are suggested for you to try, so you can actually see the answer to the question.

Some readers may want to learn about the size of the oceans, the color of ocean water, or the source of the salt in seawater. Other readers may be curious about waves, tides, or ocean currents. Information about these topics is presented in the first volume of this two-part set.

Together, the two volumes of *Incredible Facts about the Ocean* answer many questions about the biology, geology, chemistry, and physics of the ocean world. If you wish to learn more about particular ocean features or animals, see the description of the Ocean World Library books on the back cover of this book.

Continents, Islands, and Beaches

What are continents?

Continents are the six largest areas of land that separate the earth's oceans. The continents are North America, South America, Eurasia (Europe/Asia), Africa, Australia, and Antarctica. Throughout most of history, however, Europe and Asia have been considered separate continents. As a result, the world is said to have seven continents even though there are only six continental land masses. The size and location of each continent are given in Table 1.

What is a peninsula?

The word *peninsula* is used to describe a strip of land that is almost surrounded by water and attached to a larger piece of land. For example, along the south coast of Europe, the boot-shaped country of Italy is a peninsula that is nearly surrounded by the waters of the Mediterranean Sea. In the United States, Florida is a well-known peninsula. The Atlantic Ocean and the Gulf of Mexico surround much of this southern state.

Photographed from an Apollo spacecraft, the continents, oceans, and weather patterns of the earth stand out against the vast blackness of space.

Table 1. The size and location of each continent.

Continent	Approximate Surface Area		Boundaries
	square miles	square kilometers	
Eurasia			
Asia	17,000,000	44,030,000	North—Arctic Ocean East—Pacific Ocean South—Indian Ocean West—Europe and North Africa
Europe	4,000,000	10,360,000	North—Arctic Ocean East—Asia South—Mediterranean and Black seas West—Atlantic Ocean
Africa	12,000,000	31,080,000	North—Mediterranean Sea East—Indian Ocean and Asia South—Atlantic and Indian oceans West—Atlantic Ocean
North America	9,000,000	23,310,000	North—Arctic Ocean East—Atlantic Ocean South—Gulf of Mexico West—Pacific Ocean

NASA's LANDSAT-1, *an earth resources satellite, took a large number of photographs from space that were put together to produce this picture of the Italian peninsula.*

Table 1.   The size and location of each continent (continued)

| Continent | Approximate Surface Area | | Boundaries |
	square miles	square kilometers	
South America	7,000,000	18,130,000	North—Caribbean Sea East—Atlantic Ocean South—Atlantic and Pacific oceans West—Pacific Ocean
Antarctica	5,000,000	12,950,000	Surrounded by the Antarctic Ocean
Australia	3,000,000	7,770,000	North—Timor and Arafura seas East—Pacific Ocean South—Indian Ocean West—Indian Ocean
Total	57,000,000	147,630,000	

What is an isthmus?

An isthmus *(IHS-muhs)* is a narrow strip of land with water on both sides that connects two larger pieces of land. The Isthmus of Panama connects North America with South America.

What is a cape?

A cape is a point of land that extends into the ocean and is usually large enough to change the direction of currents flowing along the nearby coast. In the United States, Cape Canaveral on the east coast of Florida is the site of the Kennedy Space Center. Some capes, such as Cape of Good Hope, South Africa, are attached to larger land masses. Others, such as Cape Hatteras, North Carolina, are island capes. They are completely separate from the nearby **mainland**.*

What is an island?

An island is an area of land, smaller than a continent, that is completely surrounded by water. Some islands are very small, measuring less than 100 yards (91.4 meters) across. Others are extremely large, sometimes hundreds of miles across. The ten largest islands in the world are listed in Table 2.

*Words in **bold type** are explained in the glossary at the end of this book.

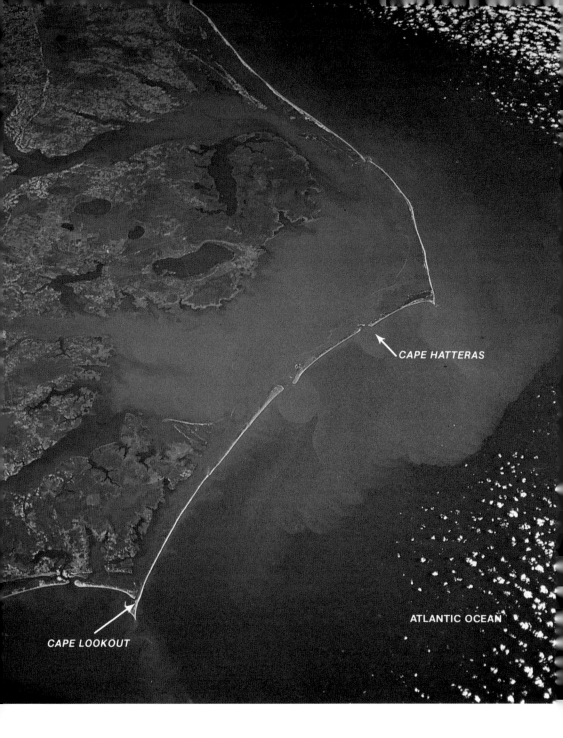

CAPE HATTERAS

CAPE LOOKOUT

ATLANTIC OCEAN

The astronauts of Apollo 9 photographed Cape Hatteras, North Carolina, as they passed far above in earth orbit.

Table 2.   The ten largest islands in the world.

Island	Approximate Surface Area		Location
	square miles	square kilometers	
1. *Greenland*	840,000	2,175,600	North Atlantic Ocean
2. *New Guinea*	306,000	792,540	South Pacific Ocean
3. *Borneo*	280,000	725,459	South Pacific Ocean
4. *Madagascar*	226,600	586,894	Indian Ocean
5. *Baffin*	196,000	507,640	Arctic Ocean
6. *Sumatra*	165,000	427,350	Indian Ocean
7. *Honshu*	88,000	227,920	Pacific Ocean
8. *Great Britain*	84,200	218,078	Atlantic Ocean
9. *Victoria*	83,900	217,301	Arctic Ocean
10. *Ellesmere*	75,700	196,063	Arctic Ocean

Hawaii, Japan, and New Zealand are well-known islands found in the Pacific Ocean. Bermuda, Cuba, and Jamaica are three islands in the Atlantic Ocean.

When an island is small, it is sometimes called an isle. But this word is not always used to describe small islands. For example, the islands that form the nation of Great Britain are also known as the British Isles.

In this view from space, Mauna Loa, a volcano on the island of Hawaii, produces fumes and steam from a river of hot lava pouring down its slopes.

How are islands made?

Some islands are formed when volcanoes on the bottom of the ocean erupt, and hot **lava** flows into the sea. As layer upon layer of lava piles up, the sides of an underwater volcano slowly become thicker and higher. When the top of the volcano becomes high enough to rise above the surface of the ocean, land is formed. This new area of land is called a volcanic island or simply an island. The Hawaiian Islands and many other islands in the Pacific Ocean were formed in this way.

Not all islands, however, are the tops of volcanoes.

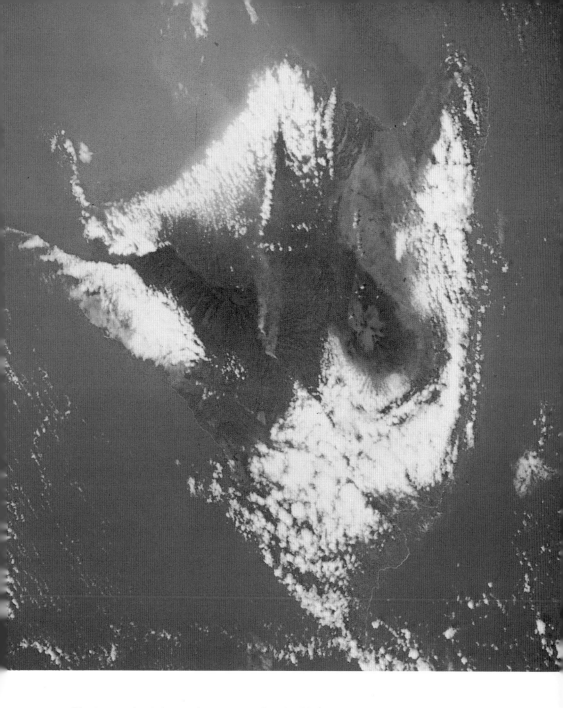

Photographed from the space shuttle Discovery, *a volcano towers over one of the Canary Islands in the Atlantic Ocean.*

Some are the tops of mountains that are mostly covered by water. These mountains do not stop at the edge of dry land. Instead, they continue out into the ocean for a short distance. Though the mountain valleys have been flooded, the peaks and ridges have remained dry and have become islands. Islands formed in this way are found along the coast of Maine, Scotland, and the northwest coast of Spain.

Sometimes ocean waves and currents actually build long, narrow strips of land called barrier islands. These islands are located **offshore** and parallel to the mainland, but not in contact with it. Barrier islands are formed by waves pushing sand up from the ocean bottom as currents bring sand from other places and add it to the pile. There are many barrier islands along the east coast of the United States and in the Gulf of Mexico, such as the Outer Banks of North Carolina and Padre Island, Texas. Atlantic City, New Jersey, Galveston, Texas, and Palm Beach, Daytona Beach, and Miami Beach, Florida, are all built on barrier islands.

What is an atoll?

An atoll *(AY tawl)* is a round, oval, or horseshoe-shaped coral island that surrounds a small body of

Viewed from an orbiting space shuttle, the coral reefs of Tarawa and Abaiang atolls of the Gilbert Islands in the Pacific Ocean surround bright, blue-green lagoons.

water called a lagoon. Atolls occur most often in the Pacific Ocean. The Cook, Gilbert, and Marshall Islands are examples of atolls.

How are atolls formed?

Atolls are formed gradually over millions of years in four basic steps. First, a volcano erupts on the bottom of the ocean and pours hot lava into the water. This lava piles up layer upon layer and then cools and hardens. Eventually, the pile of lava rises above the surface of the water and forms a small piece of land. This land is called a volcanic island.

In the second step, tiny animals called corals build their rocklike homes underwater on the sides of the volcano. Such coral homes create a "fringing reef" around the edge of the island. (See also "How are coral reefs made?" on page 82.) The island, however, does not stay this way forever. Slowly, over millions of years, the huge volcano sinks into the ocean bottom. As the volcano sinks, the coral animals build their reefs higher, keeping the top of the reefs just below the surface of the water.

During the third step, the volcano sinks down so far into the ocean bottom that only its tip can be seen

HOW AN ATOLL IS FORMED

Newly Formed Volcanic Island

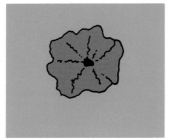 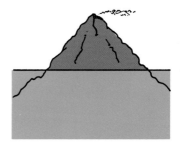

Fringing Reef

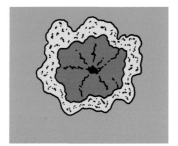 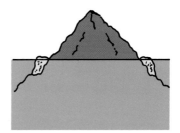

Barrier Reef

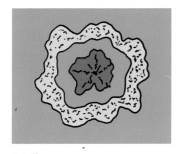 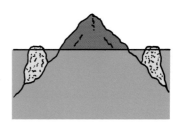

Atoll

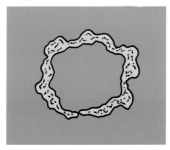 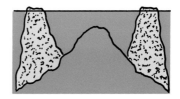

From the top of the page to the bottom, these diagrams show the four steps in which atolls are formed. The steps are shown both from a side view (right) and a top view (left).

above the water. The reef that the coral animals have built is now separated from the small island by water. This ring-shaped reef around the island is called a "barrier reef." After the volcanic island sinks completely beneath the ocean, the ring-shaped coral reef remains just below the surface of the water.

Finally, in the fourth step of building an atoll, pieces of coral are broken from the reef by the pounding of ocean waves. These pieces of coral, often weighing more than a ton, are pushed by the waves onto the top of the reef. Slowly, the pounding waves break them apart, forming coral sand. As the pieces of coral and sand continue to pile up, an island, called an atoll, forms on top of the reef.

Most atolls are found in the western Pacific Ocean where many volcanoes rise from the ocean floor. Some atolls, such as Wake, Midway, and the Marshall Islands, appear in a world atlas or on a world map. From the Hawaiian Islands, Midway lies to the north, while Wake and the Marshall Islands lie to the west.

What is a delta?

Shaped like a triangle, a delta forms where a river flows into a slow-moving body of water. Moving river

DELTAS

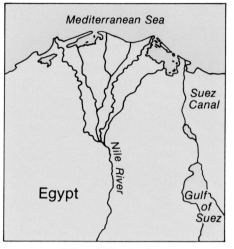

The Nile Delta

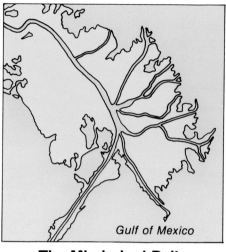

The Mississippi Delta

water can carry **sediment**, but still water cannot. As a result, soil carried along in a flowing river falls to the bottom when the water stops moving and slowly piles up to form a delta.

Deltas are often found where rivers flow into gulfs, seas, bays, or other slow-moving bodies of water. One of the largest deltas in the world lies at the mouth of the Mississippi River where its water flows into the Gulf of Mexico. Another delta has formed where the Nile River empties its sediments into the Mediterranean Sea along the north coast of Africa.

To see how moving water carries sediment, try the following experiment. First, put a tablespoon of sand (not dirt or mud) into a quart jar. Slowly add water

In this photograph, taken from the LANDSAT-1 satellite high above the earth, the huge amount of sediment carried by the Mississippi River shows up as a light-colored cloud of mud and silt at the river's mouth.

until it is about two or three inches (five to eight centimeters) from the top of the jar. Next, use a spoon to stir the sand and water very quickly for a few seconds, and then pull the spoon out of the jar. Now watch the sand in the water. While the water is spinning around, most of the sand is moving with it. But as the moving water slows down, the sand begins falling to the bottom of the jar. The larger, heavier grains are the first to fall. Soon the smaller, lighter grains sink, too, as the moving water slows even more.

What is a sandbar?

A sandbar is a long **ridge** of sand and gravel that forms beneath the surface of the water a short distance from a beach. These offshore bars, as they are sometimes called, lie parallel to the shore and usually can be seen only when the tide is extremely low.

Even though sandbars are completely underwater most of the time, you can often locate them by watching waves approach a beach. If a sandbar is beneath the water, the waves will break twice—once as they cross the bar, and again when they reach the beach. If a bar is not present, the waves will break only against the beach.

Low tide reveals this sandbar along the Maine coast. (Lynn Stone)

What is a sand spit?

The name *spit* or *sand spit* describes a long, narrow sandy beach that has one end attached to land, while the other end extends out into a body of water.

A spit is formed where swift, shallow water currents carry sand and gravel with them in the water just offshore. When these currents flow into deeper water at the entrance to a bay or harbor, they slow down and the sand that is being carried along falls to the bottom. If sand continues to pile up over a long period of time, a spit gradually forms. As long as the currents continue bringing sand, the spit becomes larger and larger.

Sand spits are found in many sizes ranging from small ones less than ten yards (nine meters) long to large spits more than nineteen miles (thirty-one kilometers) long. Two large, well-known spits lie at the entrance to New York Harbor. On the northern side is Rockaway Spit, and on the southern side of the harbor entrance is Sandy Hook.

Is all sand the same color?

No, all the sandy beaches of the world are not the same color. Some beaches are covered with bright white sand, while the sand on other beaches may be pinkish, greenish, dull white, or even black.

The color of the sand depends upon the color of the materials that formed it. In tropical areas where corals and seashells are crushed into sand, the beaches are often bright white or slightly pink in color. Where dark lava from volcanoes has been broken into tiny pieces, black or greenish-colored sands cover the beaches. Parts of the Hawaiian Islands and other Pacific islands

Sea oats stand out against dark storm clouds on a light-sand beach along the Florida coast. (Lynn Stone)

have these black sand beaches. Along the east coast of the United States, many beaches have light-colored or dull-white sand on them. Most of this sand comes from the **weathering** of granite rocks, which contain large amounts of the **mineral** quartz. Sand forms when granite rocks are broken down into tiny, sand-sized pieces. Eventually, high winds, pounding rains, and extreme hot and cold temperatures break down enough rocks to form a sand beach.

Large boulders and rocky cliffs meet the ocean on the Maine coast by the Pemaquid Lighthouse. (Lynn Stone)

What exactly is the seashore?

The seashore is the narrow strip of land right next to the ocean that comes in contact with the water. Another name for this land is "the shore." The actual line where the land and water meet is called the shoreline. Throughout the world two main kinds of seashores appear. One is the gently sloping beach, and the other is the rocky seashore where large boulders or rocky cliffs meet the ocean.

Are ocean beaches always sandy?

No, when the land along the edge of the ocean is covered with sand, gravel, or even small pieces of rock, it is called a beach. In England, for example, many beaches are made of small flat stones known as **shingle**. Along the coasts of Alaska, beaches are often covered with round stones three to eight inches (eight to twenty centimeters) across called **cobbles**. Other places have gravel beaches. The soft, sandy ocean beaches found in many parts of the world represent one particular kind of beach.

Bodies of Water in the Ocean

What is the ocean?

The ocean is the huge body of salt water that covers almost three quarters of our planet and separates the continents of the world. This world ocean is divided into the Atlantic, Pacific, Indian, Arctic, and Antarctic (or Southern) oceans. In and around these five oceans are other bodies of water such as bays, gulfs, and lagoons, all filled with salty ocean water.

Is the sea the same as the ocean?

The word *sea* is often used to mean the ocean. For example, when we say a ship is going to sea, we mean that the ship is going out on the ocean. The name sea is also given to small sections of the ocean that are partly surrounded by land. For example, the Caribbean Sea in the Atlantic Ocean is bordered to the west and south by the continents of North and South America. Some of the other major seas of the world and their locations are presented in Table 3.

Table 3. Some of the major seas of the world and their locations.

Ocean	Sea	Location
Pacific	Bering Sea	West coast of Alaska
	Coral Sea	East coast of Australia
	East China Sea	East coast of China
	Philippine Sea	East coast of the Philippine Islands
	Sea of Japan	East coast of Asia and west coast of Japan
	Sea of Okhotsk	East coast of the Soviet Union
	South China Sea	South coast of China
	Tasman Sea	Between the east coast of Australia and the west coast of New Zealand
	Yellow Sea	East coast of China
Atlantic	Baltic Sea	Along the north coast of Poland and west coast of the Soviet Union
	Black Sea	Along the north coast of Turkey
	Caribbean Sea	North coast of South America
	Mediterranean Sea	South coast of Europe, the west coast of Asia, and the north coast of Africa

Ocean	Sea	Location
	North Sea	Between the United Kingdom (England) and the European mainland
	Norwegian Sea	West coast of Norway
Indian	*Andaman Sea*	South coast of Asia
	Arabian Sea	South coast of Asia
	Red Sea	Between North Africa and Saudi Arabia
Antarctic	*Ross Sea*	Along the coast of the Antarctic continent, south of the Pacific Ocean
	Weddell Sea	Along the coast of the Antarctic continent, south of the Atlantic Ocean
Arctic	*Barents Sea*	North coasts of Norway, Sweden, Finland, and the Soviet Union
	Chukchi Sea	West coast of Alaska
	White Sea	North coast of the Soviet Union

Table 3. **Some of the major seas of the world and their locations. (continued)**

MEDITERRANEAN SEA

SUEZ CANAL

SINAI
PENINSULA

GULF OF
AQABA

GULF OF
SUEZ

ARA
PENIN

AFRICA

RED SEA

The Red Sea, which lies between northeast Africa and Saudi Arabia, is the large body of water at the bottom of this Apollo 7 photo. The Gulf of Suez and the Suez Canal connect the Red Sea to the Mediterranean Sea at the top.

Separating an ocean into smaller parts such as seas makes it much easier to locate a particular part of a huge ocean. Without these smaller parts, giving directions could be very difficult. Imagine trying to tell a friend how to get to your house if you could only give this friend the name of your continent.

What is a gulf?

A gulf is a large body of water that is partly enclosed by land. The Gulf of Mexico, along the south coast of the United States, is bordered by parts of Florida, Alabama, Mississippi, Louisiana, Texas, and Mexico. The Gulf of Saint Lawrence along the east coast of Canada, the Gulf of Carpentaria along the north coast of Australia, and the Gulf of Siam south of Thailand in Asia are partly enclosed in a similar way.

Not all of the gulfs in the world, however, look like these four. Gulfs can also be long and narrow, such as the Gulf of California, the Gulf of Finland, or the Persian Gulf. Other gulfs, such as the Gulf of Alaska, are wide bodies of water that curve into a piece of land.

Is a bay the same as a gulf?

No, a bay is not the same as a gulf, even though it is sometimes difficult to tell the difference between them.

The word *bay* is often used to describe a body of water that is partly enclosed by land, like a gulf. A bay, though, is smaller than a gulf. In addition, a bay usually has a wide mouth that is more open to the sea than the mouth of a gulf. Cape Cod Bay in Massachusetts and Monterey Bay in California have such a size and shape.

Bays not only curve into the land beside an ocean, but they are also found along the edges of lakes. If you look closely at a map showing the five Great Lakes of North America, you can find Green Bay in Lake Michigan and Georgian Bay in Lake Huron.

A very small bay may be called a **cove**. Many coves cut into the rocky coast of New England in the northeastern United States. It is in these small bays that boats find shelter from dangerous storms.

Where is the mouth of a bay?

The word *mouth* describes the place where one body of water enters another body of water. For example, the mouth of Chesapeake Bay is where the bay water meets the water of the Atlantic Ocean. In the same way, the mouth of the Mississippi River is the place where the long river ends and the Gulf of Mexico begins.

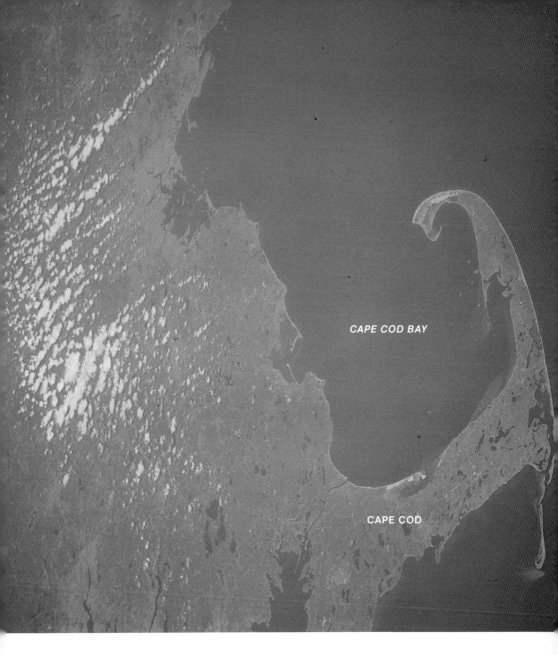

CAPE COD BAY

CAPE COD

Photographed from the space shuttle Columbia, *the narrow, curving land of Cape Cod forms the shape and mouth of Cape Cod Bay.*

What is a strait?

A strait is a narrow **waterway** or channel that connects two larger bodies of water. On a world map, it is possible to see how the narrow Strait of Gibraltar connects the Mediterranean Sea with the Atlantic Ocean. In the same way, Hudson Strait, on the east coast of Canada, connects Hudson Bay with the North Atlantic Ocean.

What is a sound?

In terms of the ocean, the word *sound* describes a long, narrow body of water that separates an island from the mainland. Along the coast of North Carolina, the Pamlico Sound separates the long strip of islands known as the Outer Banks from the mainland. In this same way, Long Island Sound lies between Long Island and New York and Connecticut on the mainland.

What is a lagoon?

A lagoon is a shallow, quiet body of water partly separated from the ocean by barriers such as sandbars or coral reefs. Narrow openings in the sandbars or the reefs allow water to flow between the lagoon and the ocean.

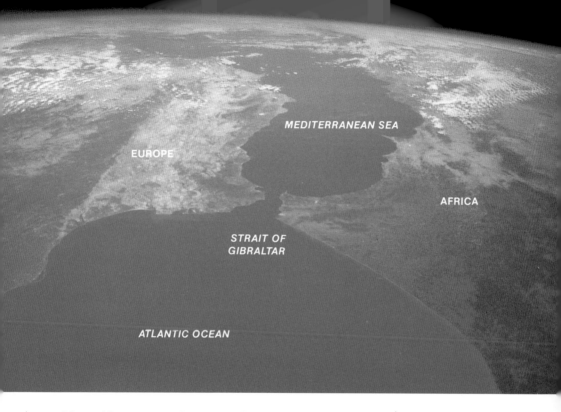

Viewed from space, the narrow Strait of Gibraltar connects the Mediterranean Sea with the Atlantic Ocean and divides Spain in Europe from Morocco in North Africa.

There are two different kinds of lagoons. One is the long, shallow, baylike body of water located behind an offshore barrier island or a group of long, narrow, sandy islands. The second kind of lagoon is the body of water within a round, oval, or horseshoe-shaped island called an atoll.

Land Beneath the Ocean

What is an "ocean basin"?

The words *ocean basin* describe the huge **depression**, or low area, in the surface of the earth that holds the water in the world's oceans. Ocean basins are separated from each other by high, dry areas of land called islands and continents.

Basins filled with water may be small as well as large. For instance, a very small depression in the ground that holds water is often called a mud puddle. If the depression is larger, it may be called a pond or lake. In the same way, water standing in the largest depressions on earth form our oceans.

Is the bottom of the ocean shaped like a basin or tub?

No, an ocean basin is not bowl-shaped like the sides of a bathtub or kitchen sink. Instead, the vast land beneath the ocean can be separated into three major parts—the continental shelf, the continental slope, and the deep-ocean floor.

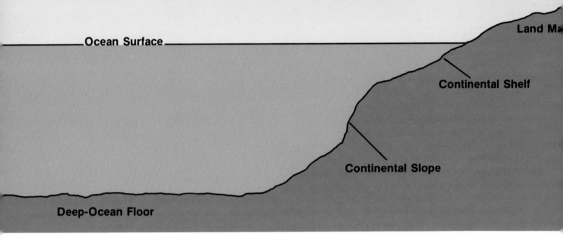

THE EDGE OF A CONTINENT

Ocean Surface

Land Ma

Continental Shelf

Continental Slope

Deep-Ocean Floor

Along the edges of the continents, the land slants gently downward beneath the ocean water. This land, known as the continental shelf, is actually a part of the continent that has become flooded by the ocean. The width of the continental shelf is not the same in all places. Along the north coast of the Soviet Union, the shelf extends almost 800 miles (1,288 kilometers) out from shore. Yet, along the west coast of South America, there are places where the continental shelf is less than one mile (1.6 kilometers) wide.

Where the gently sloping continental shelf ends, the ocean bottom drops rapidly downward. This steeply sloping land, called the continental slope, forms the bowllike sides of the ocean basin. Where the continental slope ends, the deep-ocean floor begins.

What is the ocean floor?

Ocean floor can be used to describe any of the land beneath the ocean. This land is also called the sea bottom or sea bed.

Is the land beneath the ocean sandy like a beach?

No, the land beneath the ocean is not sandy in most places. If we could remove the water from the oceans, we would find many different kinds of sediment. On the shallow, gently sloping continental shelves, the bottom is covered with either sand, mud, gravel, stones, or even bare rock. Along the continental slopes, mud and sand cover most areas. Where the slope is very steep, only bare rock may be present. On the deep-ocean floor, mud covers most of the bottom. In most places this mud is about 1000 to 2000 feet (305 to 610 meters) thick. In some places, however, the mud is only a few inches deep, while in other places, mud 10,000 feet (3,050 meters) thick has been found. That is almost 2 miles (3.2 kilometers) of mud!

Is the bottom of the ocean flat?

No, the bottom of the ocean is not flat. In fact, this land beneath the water has hills and valleys, mountains and plains, and other interesting features, just like the dry land above sea level. Some of the deepest valleys and longest mountain ranges in the world are at the bottom of the oceans. One mountain range stretches most of the way around the earth through the oceans.

Continental Shelf

Asia

Europe

Mid-Ocean
Rift

Atlantic

Ocean

Africa

Indian

Ocean

South
America

Peru-Chile
Trench

Mid-Atlantic Ridge

Mid-Indian Ri

Antarctic Ocean

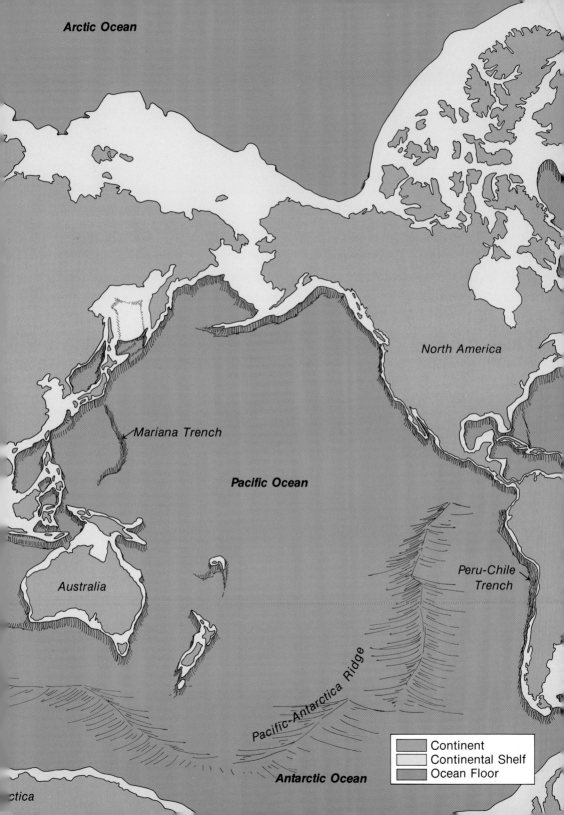

Arctic Ocean

North America

Mariana Trench

Pacific Ocean

Australia

Peru-Chile
Trench

Pacific-Antarctica Ridge

Antarctic Ocean

ctica

	Continent
	Continental Shelf
	Ocean Floor

Where are the mountains at the bottom of the ocean?

On a map of the ocean floor, a huge S-shaped mountain range rises along the center of the entire Atlantic Ocean. Because of its location, this mountain range is called the Mid-Atlantic Ridge. The long line of mountains, however, extends beyond the Atlantic Ocean. It continues around the southern tip of Africa and up into the middle of the Indian Ocean. Here the mountain range is shaped like an upside down Y, and is known as the Mid-Indian Ridge. Next, the mountains pass south of Australia and into the Pacific Ocean where they are called the Pacific-Antarctica Ridge.

From one end to the other, this enormous mountain range zig-zags along the deep-ocean floor for almost 40,000 miles (64,400 kilometers). Its peaks rise six, eight, or even ten thousand feet (3,050 meters) or more above the bottom. Since the water around these peaks is so deep, most of them are a mile or more below the ocean's surface. In only a few places do these mountain peaks rise high enough to reach the surface and form islands. One place where this happens is in the Atlantic Ocean off the coast of North Africa. Here the islands known as the Azores are actually the tops of mountains that are part of the Mid-Atlantic Ridge.

THE OCEAN BOTTOM

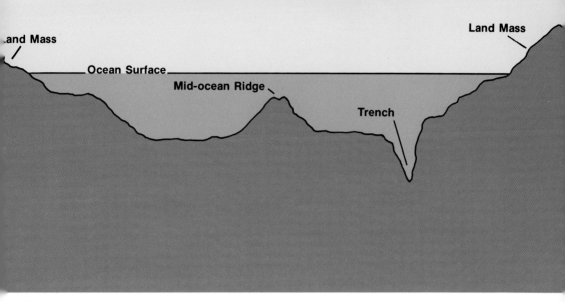

Land Mass

Land Mass

Ocean Surface

Mid-ocean Ridge

Trench

In this drawing of the ocean floor between two continents, a mid-ocean ridge and a deep ocean trench form part of the sea bottom.

What are ocean trenches?

Ocean trenches are long, deep, narrow cuts in the ocean floor. The sides or walls of these trenches are often U-shaped and very steep, plunging two, three, or even four miles (more than six kilometers) into the ocean floor. Because of their great depths, the deepest places found in the oceans are at the bottom of trenches.

You might expect the oceans to be deepest near the middle, but they are not. In fact, ocean trenches occur near the edges of continents and large groups of islands. The long, deep Peru-Chile Trench cuts into the ocean floor along the west coast of South America. Another well-known trench is found along the edge of the Mariana Islands, north of Australia. It is called the Mariana Trench. In one place, the bottom of the Mariana Trench plunges almost 7 miles (11.3 kilometers) below the ocean's surface. This is the deepest place in all the earth's oceans.

Just as the oceans have the world's longest mountain range, they also have the world's deepest valleys. Nothing on land comes close to the great depth of some ocean trenches. Even the Grand Canyon in Arizona cuts only 1 mile (1.6 kilometers) down into the earth.

What is a seamount?

A seamount is a volcano that rises from the ocean floor but does not reach the ocean's surface to form an island. These "short volcanoes" occur mainly in the Pacific and Indian oceans.

When a seamount has a flat, tablelike top, it is called a **guyot** (Gee-oh) or tablemount. A guyot is a volcano that once rose to the surface and formed an island. Over time, ocean waves and currents wore away its top, making it flat. After millions of years, the

A TABLEMOUNT

A guyot, *or tablemount, rises from the ocean floor toward the surface in this view.*

base of the volcano sank slowly into the ocean floor, leaving a flat-topped mountain far below the waves.

Have the oceans always been the shape they are now?

No, the oceans have been changing shape for millions of years because the earth's continents have been slowly moving. A map of the world as it was 225 million years ago shows one enormous piece of land surrounded by one huge ocean. This piece of land—known as *Pangaea (pan-GAY-uh)*—did not stay together. Instead, it slowly broke apart and separated

THE MOVEMENT OF THE CONTINENTS

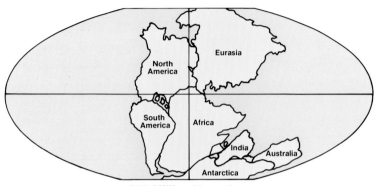

200 Million Years Ago

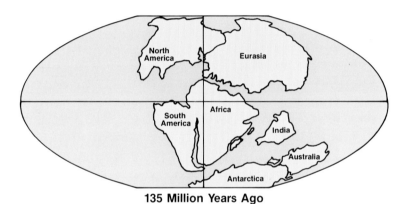

135 Million Years Ago

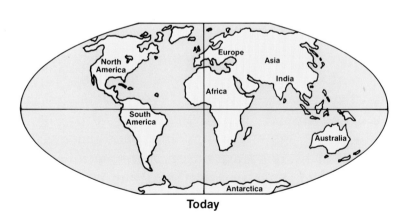

Today

into six smaller pieces of land which became the continents of the world. These six continents are known as North America, South America, Eurasia (Europe/Asia), Africa, Australia, and Antarctica. About 135 million years ago the continents were separate, but still much closer together than they are now. Not until about 30 million years ago did the continents finally move close to where they are now.

By looking closely at a map of the world today, you may be able to see how the six separate continents could fit back together like the pieces of a puzzle. You may even want to cut the shapes of each continent out of paper and try to fit them all together into one large piece. Starting with this single mass of land, Pangaea, you can slide the six continents slowly apart until they are in their current positions on a map of today's world.

Is the shape of the ocean still changing?

Yes, even now the Atlantic Ocean is slowly getting larger as North and South America continue to drift farther away from Europe and Africa. These continents, however, move very slowly and will drift only about 1 inch (2.5 centimeters) apart each year.

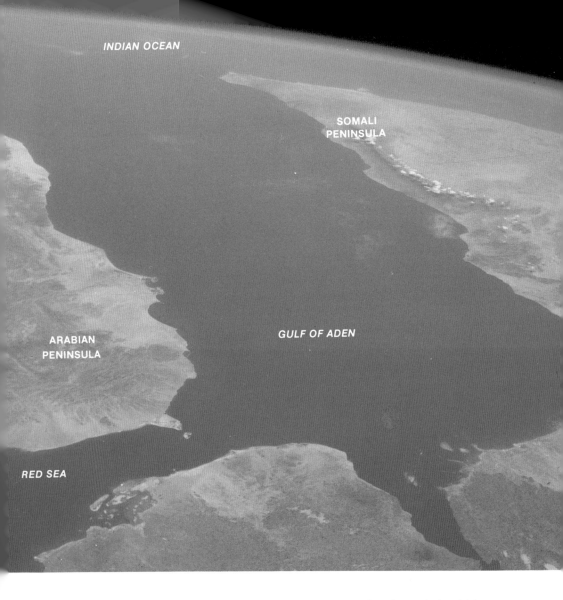

INDIAN OCEAN

SOMALI
PENINSULA

ARABIAN
PENINSULA

GULF OF ADEN

RED SEA

In this space shuttle photo of the Arabian Peninsula and the African
continent, separated by the Gulf of Aden and the Red Sea, you can see
that the two large land masses were once one and have slowly drifted
apart.

What makes the continents move?

Scientists believe that rock deep beneath the oceans and continents is so hot that it actually flows. As this rock slowly flows about, it pulls the ocean floor apart and moves the continents. The movement creates a long crack down the middle of the ocean floor. To see this crack, look at a map showing the S-shaped Mid-Atlantic Ridge in the center of the Atlantic Ocean. Now, look very closely at the high peaks along the center of this line of mountains. There you will find a deep crack or groove that runs the entire length of the mountain range. This groove is called the Mid-Ocean Rift. Hot lava forces its way up through the Mid-Ocean Rift as the ocean floor is slowly torn apart.

This gradual spreading of the ocean floor and separation of the continents is called either "seafloor spreading" or "continental drift."

4 Plants in the Ocean

What a. the nall st plants living in the ocean?

Many differer kinds of tiny plants live at the surface of the ocea Rather than staying in one place like a tree or a bush, the e plants float freely in the water and go where the oc an currents take them. This group of tiny, free-floatin plants is called **phytoplankton**. Most are so small that they can be seen only with the aid of a **microscope.**

Beautiful, **microscopic** plants known as **diatoms** are the most abundant kinds of phytoplankton living in the oceans. Even though they are tiny, these plants are an important source of food for many ocean fish.

What is seaweed?

Seaweed is the name often used to describe the large, easy-to-see plants that grow in the ocean. Many different types of seaweed can be found near the shore attached to rocks, piles, seawalls, and even on the bottom of boats. These plants have such names as sea

Large kelp plants, which appear to be green in this underwater view, are one of the many types of seaweed that grow in the world's oceans.

EXAMPLES OF PHYTOPLANKTON

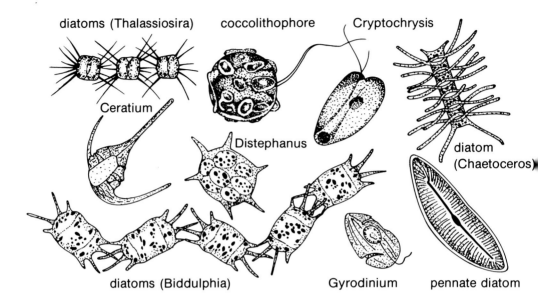

diatoms (Thalassiosira)   coccolithophore   Cryptochrysis

Ceratium

Distephanus

diatom (Chaetoceros)

diatoms (Biddulphia)   Gyrodinium   pennate diatom

lettuce, sea moss, sargassum, sea palm, rockweed, and Irish moss.

What are algae?

Algae are the thousands of plants that have no true roots, stems, or leaves and usually live in the water. These plants are divided into two major groups: the tiny, microscopic phytoplankton, and the large, **macroscopic** seaweeds.

Are all of the plants in the ocean green?

No, not all ocean plants have a green color. The large plants called seaweeds are divided into three different groups depending on their color. These plants are known as the green, red, or brown algae.

These green plants, of the species halimeda, *grow in the Red Sea and are one example of the many types of algae. (Jeff Rotman)*

It is not always possible to identify algae just by looking at the color of a plant. Knowing the color may sometimes be helpful, but it is often necessary to use a microscope to identify a particular type of plant. A trained person can look closely at the cells in one of these plants and know for sure if it is a red, green, or brown alga. (The word *algae* is plural and refers to many different kinds of these plants; *alga* is singular and used to describe only one particular kind of plant.)

What is kelp?

Kelp is the name used to describe some types of large, brown seaweeds that grow mainly along rocky coasts in the cooler waters of the ocean. These plants have such names as giant kelp, elk kelp, and bull kelp.

Even though some large kelp plants appear to have roots, stems, and leaves, they do not. Since kelps are algae, they do not have true roots, stems, or leaves. As a result, different names are used to describe these parts of a kelp plant. The lower part, which looks like roots, is called the holdfast. The stemlike portion of a kelp plant is called the stipe, and the leaflike part the blade.

What is the biggest plant that grows in the ocean?

Giant kelp is the largest plant growing in the ocean. This plant not only grows large, but it can also grow very fast. A single giant kelp plant may reach 200 feet (61 meters) in length, growing as much as two feet (61 centimeters) in a single day. Huge numbers of these plants grow together in large areas known as kelp beds along the west coast of the United States.

Do plants in the ocean need light to help them grow?

Yes, ocean plants must have sunlight in order to

Fish swim among giant kelp plants near the Santa Barbara Islands off the coast of southern California. (Charles Arneson)

grow. Like the grasses in a field, ocean plants need the energy in sunlight to help them make their own food. This food is made from two abundant substances, water and carbon dioxide, a gas. While water surrounds an ocean plant, carbon dioxide is produced when fish and other animals breathe underwater. When the sun is shining, **chlorophyll** in the cells of a plant uses the sun's energy to change water and carbon dioxide into sugar and oxygen. The sugar is the plant's food, while the oxygen is released into the water.

The following experiment will allow you to see the oxygen that a plant makes. First, go to a pet shop where tropical fish are sold and buy a couple of healthy, green aquarium plants. Take the plants home, put them in a small jar of water, and set the jar on a sunny windowsill. After a few hours return to the jar and look closely at the plants. You should be able to see small air bubbles rising up from them. These bubbles are the oxygen made by the plants. If your plants are not producing bubbles, wait a little longer, or turn on an electric lamp near the jar to give the plants more light.

Without light, plants would die. Without plants, animals, including human beings, could not live on earth. Plants give us food to eat and oxygen to breathe.

PHOTOSYNTHESIS

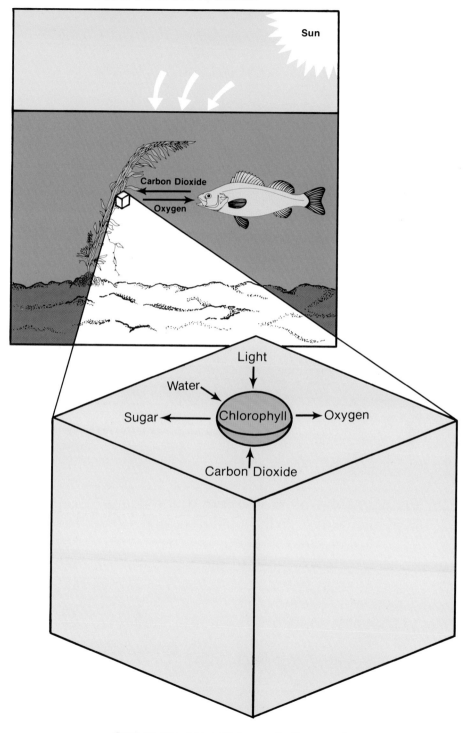

Carbon Dioxide + Water ⟶ Sugar + Oxygen

Chlorophyll in the cells of these sea grass and kelp plants use the sun's energy to change water and carbon dioxide into sugar for food and oxygen that is released into the surrounding water. (Jeff Rotman)

Do any plants live on the bottom of the ocean?

Yes, some plants do live on the ocean bottom. These plants, however, need sunlight in order to grow. As a result, they can live only in places where this light reaches the ocean bottom.

The world ocean has an average depth of 13,000 feet (3,965 meters), which is about 2.5 miles (4.4 kilometers) deep. And yet, with all this water, most plants can live only in the top 300 feet (91.5 meters) of ocean

*Some fish, such as this parrotfish in the Red Sea, feed on seaweeds.
(Jeff Rotman)*

water—the length of a single football field. Below a
depth of 300 feet, there is usually not enough light for
the plants to make their own food.

Do fish eat the plants in the ocean?

Yes, some fish graze on ocean plants, just as cows
and horses graze in grassy fields on dry land. Fish such
as menhaden feed on phytoplankton, while seaweeds
are often eaten by parrotfish.

Ocean plants are important to fish in other ways, too. The plants produce oxygen that fish breathe. Also, many different kinds of fish swim among the large seaweeds to hide from their enemies.

Is any seaweed poisonous?

A few kinds of seaweeds are not safe for people to eat. Of these, only the blue-green alga known as *Lyngbya* is actually dangerous to eat. This plant contains chemicals that could poison a person. One other less dangerous kind of seaweed is a brown alga known as *Desmarestia.* If eaten, it could cause an upset stomach.

Most other seaweeds are not dangerous if eaten. Many of these plants are eaten every day by people all over the world. Since there are a few dangerous kinds of seaweeds, though, you should not eat any of these plants until you know for sure which ones are safe.

What is the Sargasso Sea and where is it found?

The Sargasso Sea is a large area in the Atlantic Ocean where great numbers of a seaweed called *Sargassum* float in clumps at the surface of the water. This sea gets its name from these plants.

Sargassum, also called gulfweed, is an interesting

brown algae. In the Sargasso Sea, these plants branch, like a small bush, and have tiny "berries" and leaves with jagged edges along each branch. The leaves are called blades, and the "berries" are actually filled with air to keep the plants afloat. If these plants could not float, there would not be a Sargasso Sea. The plants would sink deep into the ocean where there is no sunlight and would soon die.

To locate the boundaries of the Sargasso Sea, look at a map of the Atlantic Ocean. Draw a line from the mouth of the Chesapeake Bay, in Virginia, straight across the ocean to Spain. This line marks the northern edge of the sea. Next, draw a line from Cuba, which is south of Florida, across the ocean to Africa. This line runs along the southern boundary of the Sargasso Sea. A careful look at your map will show that the top line is near a **latitude** of thirty-five degrees, while the bottom line is near a latitude of twenty degrees. Between these two lines lies the oval-shaped Sargasso Sea. It begins about 1,000 miles (1,610 kilometers) off the coast of the United States and stretches more than halfway across the Atlantic Ocean.

Ocean Animals Without Backbones— The Invertebrates

What are some of the smallest animals living in the ocean?

Many different kinds of tiny animals live in the oceans. All are part of an important group of animals known as **zooplankton**, which means "wandering animal." Zooplankton are so small that they cannot swim through the ocean. Instead, they drift in the water and go where the ocean currents take them.

Some zooplankton are tiny one-celled animals that can be seen only with the aid of a microscope. Two examples of these tiny animals, which have rather large names, are **foraminiferans** and **radiolarians**. These are among the smallest and most abundant animals found in ocean water.

Other larger members of the zooplankton community include the tiny eggs and young of animals such as fish, crabs, clams, and snails. Many are so small that they can easily pass through the eye of a needle. Before long, though, these young animals grow larger and can

EXAMPLES OF ZOOPLANKTON

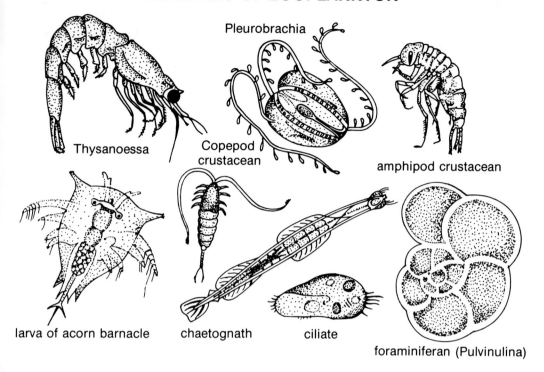

Thysanoessa

Pleurobrachia

Copepod crustacean

amphipod crustacean

larva of acorn barnacle

chaetognath

ciliate

foraminiferan (Pulvinulina)

no longer be called zooplankton. Some, such as the clams and snails, settle to the bottom where they spend the rest of their lives. Others, like the fish and crabs, become strong enough to swim through the ocean in search of food and safety.

Is a sponge really an animal?

Yes, sponges are animals that spend most of their lives in one place, firmly attached to rocks, pilings, corals, or other hard objects in the water. Most sponges live in warm, shallow, tropical water. Some can also be found in cold water, some in deep water, and a few even live in freshwater rivers, lakes, and ponds. Many of the "sponges" sold in stores today, though, are not true sponges. Instead, they are artificial sponges which only

look like the real animals that live in the ocean.

A true sponge is a remarkable animal. It has no head, mouth, stomach, or any of the other body parts most animals have. In order to stay alive, a sponge must keep water constantly moving through its body. Seawater enters the sponge through millions of tiny holes, or pores, in the skin. The water then flows through narrow canals and into small spaces, or chambers. These are lined with special cells, each having a long, hairlike tail called a **flagellum**. As the tails whip around in millions of tiny chambers, water moves through the animal's body. Within these chambers food is filtered from the water, and oxygen is absorbed into the living cells. From here, the water passes through larger canals on its way out of the sponge's body. As it passes out of the sponge, more enters through the pores in the skin, and the flow of water continues.

When you see a true sponge dried and sitting on a shelf, you are looking at the animal's skeleton. The living cells that moved the water and used the food once covered this skeleton, but they have been removed. Still, by looking at the holes in a sponge, you can see where water once flowed through the animal's body.

This brightly colored vase sponge grows on a shipwreck near the Cayman Islands in the Caribbean Sea. (Jeff Rotman)

Because sponges are so different from all other animals, scientists have placed them in a group by themselves. They are grouped together in the **phylum Porifera**. This word describes the sponges well because it means "pore bearing" animals.

Do all sponges look the same?

Even though most people think all sponges look alike, they do not. More than 5,000 different kinds of sponges of many different sizes, colors, and shapes live in the ocean.

Sponges can be very small or rather large. The smallest are less than 1 inch (2.5 centimeters) across when they are fully grown. Others, such as the logger-head sponge, can grow much larger, sometimes reaching a diameter of 3 to 4 feet (0.9 to 1.2 meters).

Sponges are also very colorful animals when they are alive. Some are red, orange, black, or brown, while others may be purple, yellow, or green.

Sponges have different shapes, too. The chicken liver sponge and fire sponge grow low and flat, covering a stone or piece of wood like paint. The red finger sponge and the yellow tube sponge have tall, narrow bodies, just as their names indicate. Some other

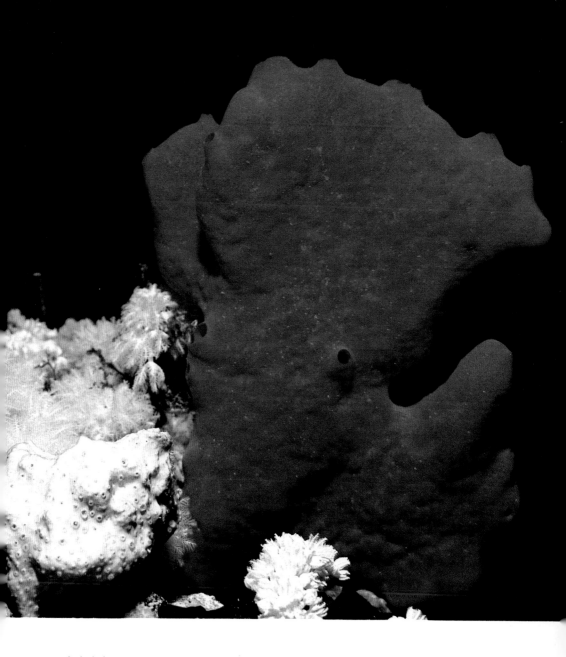

A bright-orange sponge grows among white coral in the Red Sea. Sponges come in many different sizes, colors, and shapes. (Jeff Rotman)

sponges have names that describe what they look like, too. The orange softball sponge has a round, ball-shaped body. The stinking vase sponge looks like a vase and smells very bad when brought above the water.

What is a jellyfish?

Jellyfish is a name used to describe about 200 different kinds of ocean animals with delicate, jellylike bodies. These animals live throughout the ocean world—from the icy waters surrounding the North and South poles to the warm tropical waters at the equator.

Most jellyfish have umbrella-shaped bodies that measure between 1 and 16 inches (2.5 to 40 centimeters) across. Their bodies may be colorless and glassy-looking, or they may display beautiful shades of such colors as red, orange, and purple.

Below the umbrella body, sometimes called a bell, hang threadlike **tentacles** used to sting the prey on which the animals feed. On some jellyfish these tentacles may be very short and hard to see. The tentacles of others can reach more than 100 feet (30.5 meters) down into the ocean. Though many jellyfish have a weak sting that most people cannot feel, some can cause

At home in the tropical waters of the Red Sea, this umbrella shaped, glassy-looking jellyfish has tentacles that are difficult to see. (Jeff Rotman)

serious stings. These are very painful and can even kill the unfortunate victim.

Jellyfish have some well-known relatives that include the corals and the beautiful sea anemones. While these animals may look quite different from one another, they are alike in at least one important way. Their mouths are surrounded by tentacles armed with tiny stinging cells, which no other animals have. Because of these special cells, the corals, anemones, and jellyfish are all members of the phylum **Cnidaria**. This name comes from the word *cnidocyte* (NID-oh-syt), the place where stinging cells are formed on the bodies of these animals.

How do jellyfish sting?

Jellyfish, and all their relatives, have tiny stinging cells that are usually lined up along tentacles around their mouths. Each stinging cell is filled with a liquid and a coiled, hollow tube with a very sharp point. On the outside of these cells is a small, hairlike trigger. Once the trigger is touched, the top of the stinging cell opens, and the coiled, hollow tube inside quickly shoots out. The sharp, spearlike point at the end of the tube sticks in the skin of the jellyfish's victim. The liquid, which causes the painful sting, then passes through the tube from the stinging cell and into the victim.

When a person swims into the tentacles of these animals, millions of stinging cells may be touched. All of these cells then release their tiny, poisonous darts at once. But you do not have to be a swimmer to get stung. Even jellyfish that have washed ashore can be dangerous and should not be handled. It is possible to receive a painful sting from stinging cells that are lying on a beach.

If you are ever stung by one of these animals, remove the parts of the tentacles that are stuck to you as soon as possible. To do this, use a stick, a clump of seaweed, or some other object so that your fingers and hands are not also stung. Try to avoid rubbing the injured area because some of the stinging cells on your skin may not have opened and released their poison. Rubbing will only force them open and make your injury worse. If possible, sprinkle vinegar, alcohol, baking soda, or meat tenderizer over the injured area. Any of these common items will help destroy the stinging liquid that is causing the pain. For someone who is in extreme pain, see a doctor at once for the proper treatment.

Photographed off the coast of New England, the umbrellalike bell of a Lion's Mane jellyfish has tentacles that can reach more than 100 feet (30.5 meters) hanging beneath it. (Jeff Rotman)

What are some of the most dangerous jellyfish in the oceans?

One of the most dangerous jellyfish is also the largest. It is known by at least three names: Lion's Mane, sea blubber, and pink jellyfish. This animal lives mainly in the cold waters of the North Atlantic and Arctic oceans. When fully grown, one of these jellyfish can have an umbrellalike bell that measures more than

6 feet (1.8 meters) across with tentacles more than 100 feet (30.5 meters) long hanging beneath it.

Despite its size, the Lion's Mane is not the most feared jellyfish in the world. Of the 200 different kinds of jellyfish living in the oceans, the most dangerous are the sea wasps. These animals, found in the Pacific Ocean along the coast of northern Australia, are only a few inches across. Yet, their poison is so powerful that some of the people who have come in contact with a sea wasp have died less than twenty minutes after being stung.

What is a Portuguese man-of-war?

The Portuguese man-of-war is a beautiful, interesting, and unusual ocean creature. It is not a true jellyfish, and it is not just one animal. Instead, the man-of-war is a colony of animals that must live and work together in order to survive.

Each individual in the colony has a job to do. One forms the bubblelike bladder that is filled with air and floats on the surface of the water. This float is colored in shades of blue and red, and it is usually 10 to 15 inches (25 to 38 centimeters) long. Hanging beneath the float are groups of individual animals that form long, beautiful tentacles. The tentacles may reach 50 to 100 feet (15.3 to 30.5 meters) down into the ocean. Some of these individuals are responsible for capturing food, others digest the food, and another special group produces the young.

Portuguese men-of-war can be found floating in tropical ocean water around the world. They can be dangerous as well as beautiful. The poison in many of the tentacles that hang below the harmless float makes these animals among the most dangerous invertebrates—animals without backbones—in the ocean.

What is a coral reef?

A coral reef is a hard, rocklike ridge built in warm, shallow ocean water by billions of tiny animals known as corals. Reef-building coral animals can survive only where the temperature of the water around them stays above seventy degrees Fahrenheit (twenty-one degrees Centigrade). Because of this need for warm water, most living coral reefs are found within a latitude of thirty degrees north and south of the equator.

There are three different kinds of coral reefs in the oceans. The first, called a fringing reef, is located along the edge of the shore, attached to the land. Because of

A school of goldfish swims among the cracks and crevices of a coral reef in the Red Sea. Coral reefs serve as homes in the sea for many forms of ocean life. (Jeff Rotman)

its location, you can often walk onto a fringing reef directly from the shore. The second kind of reef is known as a barrier reef, and it is separated from nearby land by a channel of water. In order to reach a barrier reef, you must swim or take a boat from the beach out to the reef. The third kind of reef is a ring- or horseshoe-shaped reef called an atoll. A small body of water known as a lagoon lies in the center of this type of reef.

How are coral reefs made?

Coral reefs are built by tiny, soft-bodied animals known as corals. These coral animals **secrete**, or release, a hard covering around their soft, delicate bodies to help protect themselves from their enemies. It is this hard covering that forms coral reefs.

When a young coral animal finds a hard surface on which to live, it secretes a material called **calcium carbonate** beneath its body. The calcium carbonate hardens like a cement floor. Here the coral animal must spend the rest of its life. The animal then secretes a wall of calcium carbonate around its body. When finished, the coral has built a hard, cup-shaped fortress in which to live. At the same time, the animal has also built a tiny part of a huge coral reef.

Each individual coral animal, known as a **polyp**, has a body that looks like a tiny peanut butter jar. The top of a coral polyp's body is surrounded by tentacles, covered with tiny stinging cells. At night these tentacles wave about in the water. They capture bits of food that are passed through a slitlike mouth into the polyp. During the day, however, the polyp slips down into the safety of its protective cup to avoid its enemies.

When you see a piece of coral displayed on a shelf, you are not seeing the animal. You are looking at the calcium carbonate skeletons made by hundreds of tiny coral polyps that have lived and died.

For millions of years, tiny coral animals have helped change the face of the earth. Their coral reefs slow down powerful ocean waves and help protect nearby land from being destroyed. When volcanoes erupt and form new islands, corals build reefs around the edges of the island and help prevent erosion, or wearing away, of the land. When the hard coral finally does break apart, it is pounded by ocean waves into fine sand that covers tropical beaches. In these and many other ways, coral animals have helped change the appearance of our world. Their work continues today in places where pollution has not destroyed them.

What are shellfish?

The word *shellfish* is used to describe many different kinds of animals that live in water and have shells covering their bodies. Some of the most easily recognized shell-covered animals in the ocean are clams and snails. Crabs, lobsters, and shrimps also have shell-covered bodies, and they, too, are called shellfish. And yet, even though all of these animals have shells, none of them are really fish. (See also "What is a fish?" on page 103.)

What are seashells?

Seashells are the hard, protective homes built by soft-bodied animals such as clams and snails. It is often possible to identify these shells and know who built them. For example, clams usually build two-piece seashells that are hinged together. Snails, though, build one-piece shells that are often spiral-shaped. Other seashell builders include chitons that have eight-piece shells, chambered nautiluses that have one-piece shells with several rooms called chambers, and tusk shell builders whose shells look like tiny elephant tusks. Each of these seashell home builders is part of the large group of animals known as **mollusks**.

A spiny lobster moves along the ocean bottom off the coast of California. (Jeff Rotman)

A colorful giant clam, perhaps weighing as much as 500 pounds (227 kilograms), lives among fire coral in the Red Sea. (Jeff Rotman)

How big is a giant clam?

Some giant clams may grow more than 4 feet (1.2 meters) across and weigh more than 500 pounds (227 kilograms). Each half of a clam shell this size can weigh as much as a large man. No other mollusk in the world comes close to building such a huge shell.

Are an octopus and a squid the same animal?

No, an octopus and a squid are not the same animal, but they are very closely related to one another. Even though these animals are similar in many ways, it is not difficult to tell them apart. The body of an octopus is round, soft, and baglike. It has a head that extends outward, forming eight long arms. Each arm is lined along one side with suction cups that are used to capture and hold food. A squid, on the other hand, has a long, slender, cigar-shaped body with ten long arms extending from its head. Two of these arms have suction cups only at the tip ends, while the other eight arms have the cups for their entire length.

Frightening stories have been told about huge octopuses that wrap their arms around ships and pull them beneath the ocean's surface. But these are just stories. Most of these animals are small, measuring only a few feet from the tip of one arm to the tip of an arm on the opposite side of the body. Some of the largest octopuses live in the Pacific Ocean and have arms that reach 16 feet (4.8 meters) in length. Their bodies are slightly larger than a football. While an octopus this size may be able to hold a person underwater, it could not pull a ship below the surface. Much larger octopuses may live

An octopus, with eight long arms extending outward from its head, stands out against the dark sea around it. (Jeff Rotman)

in the deep ocean, but so far none have been found.

Some giant squids, though, may truly be called ocean monsters. These animals grow to 60 feet (18.3 meters) in length and attack sperm whales in the dark water thousands of feet below the ocean's surface. The suction cup marks left by squids on the heads of some whales indicate that giant squids may grow 150 to 200 feet (45.1 to 61 meters) in length.

Off the coast of New England, the slender, cigar-shaped body of a squid has ten arms which extend from its head. (Jeff Rotman)

The octopus and the squid are mollusks that do not have hard shells covering their soft bodies. Their closest relatives are the snails and the clams.

Can an octopus or a squid swim?

Yes, both octopuses and squids are excellent swimmers. But instead of using fins to move themselves through the water, these animals use "jet power."

To swim, an octopus or squid allows a special chamber inside of its body to fill with water through a large opening. Once full, this large opening is shut. Then, using special muscles, the animal quickly forces the water out of its body through a small narrow tube called a funnel. As the water rushes out, the animal moves swiftly forward. An octopus or a squid can change its direction by pointing the funnel in the direction opposite to the way it wants to go.

You can see how this water jet works by blowing air into a balloon and letting it go. As the air rushes out, the balloon is pushed ahead in the opposite direction.

What are horseshoe crabs?

Horseshoe crabs, also known as king crabs, are slow-moving animals that have lived in the oceans for more than 300 million years. These animals crawled in shallow ocean waters when the continents began drifting apart to form the Atlantic Ocean. Horseshoe crabs lived in the oceans when the dinosaurs roamed the earth. They are still here today and look very much the same as they did long ago.

The body of a horseshoe crab can be divided into three parts: a head, a hind-body called the **abdomen**, and a long, spikelike tail. The horseshoe-shaped head gives the animal its name. If the animal is turned onto its back, you can see its legs and gills. Its mouth is located between the two rows of legs, which have joints where they can bend. Horseshoe crabs and all other animals with jointed legs are members of the enormous phylum known as **arthropods**.

Horseshoe crabs live in shallow ocean water where they crawl along the bottom in search of food. They eat algae, clams, and other small animals.

Horseshoe crabs are not true crabs at all. In fact, these animals are more closely related to spiders and scorpions. You can observe one characteristic that separates the true crabs from the horseshoe crabs. If you look closely at a crab, or one of its relatives such as a lobster, a shrimp, or a crayfish, you can see two pairs of **antennae**, or "feelers," on the animal's head. But the head of a horseshoe crab, like the head of a spider or scorpion, has no antennae.

Is a starfish really a fish?

No, a starfish is not a fish, but it is a star-shaped animal that lives in the sea. These animals, then, are more accurately called "sea stars."

Most sea stars have a small body that is surrounded, like a star, by at least five arms. It is not unusual, though, for these animals to have more than five arms. Some have as many as forty arms, and a few may have even more.

About 1,500 different kinds of sea stars live in the oceans of the world. Most of these animals are between 6 and 9 inches (15 to 22.5 centimeters) across, but some are very small, only 0.5 inch (1.3 centimeters) wide when fully grown. Others, such as the sunflower star, may grow quite large, reaching 3 or 4 feet (0.9 to 1.2 meters) across.

Sea stars have some very well known relatives such as sea urchins and sand dollars. This group of animals is called the **echinoderms**, a word that means "spiny-skinned" animals. The spiny skin is easy to see on animals such as sea urchins. On some of the other echinoderms, though, you must look very closely to see the skin's roughness. The surface of a living sand dollar, for instance, is "furry" or "fuzzy." These tiny little "spines" have often been scraped or worn away when we find one of these animals washed up on a beach.

The five arms of a candy cane sea star rest on coral in the Red Sea. (Jeff Rotman)

Ocean Animals With Backbones— The Vertebrates

What is the biggest animal living in the ocean?

The blue whale is by far the largest animal in our oceans. These giants often grow to a length of 100 feet (30.5 meters) and may weigh as much as 200 tons (181.4 metric tons). It is hard to imagine that a single animal could be so large and weigh more than 2,000 grown men.

These huge animals do not eat large sea creatures. Instead, blue whales eat mostly very small, shrimplike animals that are filtered from the water. For a blue whale, a mouthful of food can weigh as much as 100 pounds (45 kilograms). In a single day, one of these giants can eat as much as 9,000 pounds (4,086 kilograms) of food.

Blue whales are not only the largest animals in the oceans today. They are the largest animals that have ever lived on earth—in the water or on land. These whales are even larger than any of the dinosaurs that once roamed our planet.

Near the coast of Alaska, the tail of a diving whale shows its telltale fluke marks. Thousands of whales feed on tiny, shrimplike animals called krill in these northern waters.

How big is a baby blue whale?

Not even a baby blue whale is small. At birth this animal is about twenty-three feet (seven meters) long and weighs almost 4,400 pounds (1,998 kilograms). That's more than two tons!

Whales are **warm-blooded**, air-breathing mammals that maintain a steady body temperature. Like other mammals, a baby whale is fed milk from special glands in its mother's body. A blue whale's mother, though, has a job like no other mother. Her two-ton baby, called a calf, can drink more than 130 gallons (491 liters) of milk each day. With this supply of milk, the calf gains about 200 pounds (91 kilograms) of weight each day. After eight to ten months, the young animal stops nursing and must find its own food.

If the young whale stays healthy and is not killed by another sea creature or by a harpoon from a whaling ship, then its life can be a long one. Although no one knows how long a blue whale lives, scientists believe these beautiful animals can live more than 100 years.

Do all whales have teeth?

Whales are easily separated into two groups: those with teeth, called the toothed whales, and those without teeth, called the toothless whales. While the whales with teeth may eat fish, squid, seals, and other large sea animals, the toothless whales cannot. Instead, they eat the tiny plants and animals, called plankton, that float in the water around them.

In place of teeth, the toothless whales have strips of **baleen** in their mouths that trap the small food they eat. The baleen is made of a strong flexible material similar to that of human fingernails. When the animal opens its large mouth, water flows in, carrying food with it. The mouth is then closed and the water forced out, leaving the tiny plankton trapped in the baleen. Because of the way in which toothless whales feed, they are also called baleen whales.

Does a whale blow water out of a hole on the top of its head?

A whale does not really blow water out of a hole on the top of its head. Whales are air-breathing animals, and this hole allows the air they need to pass to and from their lungs. The hole, then, is similar to the nose on a person's face.

The "water" that comes from the head of a whale is actually a cloud of steam. Such a cloud forms when a

EXAMPLES OF WHALES IN THE OCEANS

Bowhead Whale
Balaena mysticetus
Up to 60 feet
(18 meters) long
Baleen

Narwhal
Monodon monoceros
Up to 15 feet
(5 meters) long
Toothed

Beluga
Delphinapterus leucas
Up to 15 feet
(5 meters) long
Toothed

Black Right Whale
Eubalaena glacialis
Up to 60 feet
(18 meters) long
Baleen

Sei Whale
Balaenoptera borealis
Up to 55 feet
(17 meters) long
Baleen

Fin Whale
Balaenoptera physalus
Up to 80 feet
(24 meters) long
Baleen

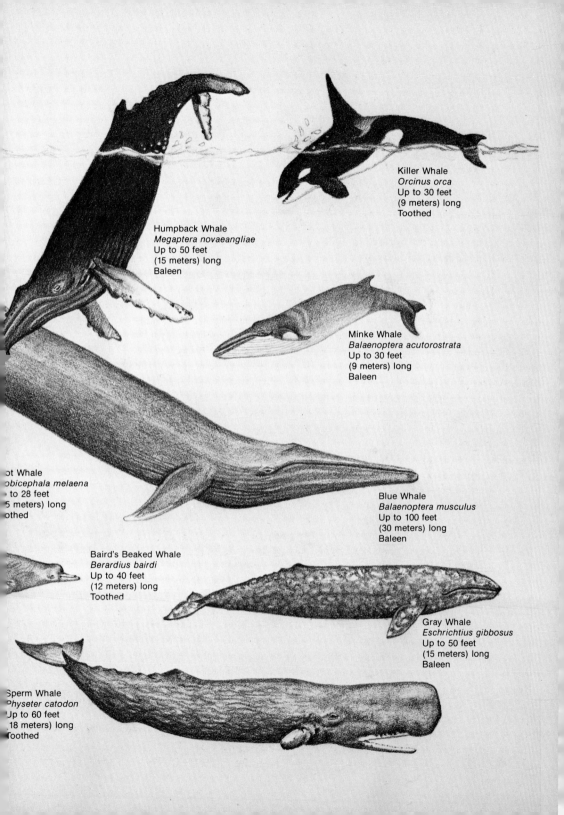

Killer Whale
Orcinus orca
Up to 30 feet
(9 meters) long
Toothed

Humpback Whale
Megaptera novaeangliae
Up to 50 feet
(15 meters) long
Baleen

Minke Whale
Balaenoptera acutorostrata
Up to 30 feet
(9 meters) long
Baleen

ot Whale
obicephala melaena
to 28 feet
5 meters) long
othed

Blue Whale
Balaenoptera musculus
Up to 100 feet
(30 meters) long
Baleen

Baird's Beaked Whale
Berardius bairdi
Up to 40 feet
(12 meters) long
Toothed

Gray Whale
Eschrichtius gibbosus
Up to 50 feet
(15 meters) long
Baleen

Sperm Whale
Physeter catodon
Up to 60 feet
(18 meters) long
Toothed

Rising to the surface to breathe, a whale blows a large amount of warm, moist air out of its lungs.

whale comes to the surface and quickly blows a large amount of warm, moist air out of its lungs. The air quickly cools once it is outside of the whale's warm body. As it cools, the moisture in the air **condenses** and appears as a white cloud of steam over the whale's head. This cloud is called the blow or the spout.

Do some whales have horns on their heads?

One whale called a narwhal *(NAHR-wuhl)*, living in the icy waters of the Arctic Ocean, looks as if a horn is growing on its head. The "horn," though, is really a long, spiral-shaped tooth called a tusk. This tusk usually grows out from the left jaw of the male narwhals and does not appear on females or young whales.

The body of a full-grown male narwhal can be 15 feet (4.6 meters) long, with a tusk that may reach a length of 10 feet (3 meters). This long, single tusk is probably used as a weapon when these whales get into fights. But it has another use, too. The tusk quickly lets other narwhals know which animals are the males.

What is a sea cow?

A sea cow is a large, air-breathing mammal that lives in shallow, tropical waters around the world. It grazes on underwater plants as a cow grazes in grassy fields on land.

The name *sea cow* actually describes two different, but very similar, animals—manatees and dugongs. Both of these animals have large, thick, streamlined bodies with broad, flat, paddlelike tails. Their tails, like the tails of a whale or porpoise, move up and down to push them through the water. Their two front legs are also flat and paddle-shaped and help them move in their watery world. Sea cows are so well built for their lives in the water that if one of them is stranded on land, it is unable to crawl back to the water.

In the past, some sailors thought the large sea cows were beautiful mermaids. It is hard to understand how the story got started, but even now there are people who talk of mermaids living in the oceans.

Today, these friendly, gentle animals are almost **extinct**. Like so many other animals, sea cows have been hunted and killed by people in such large numbers that soon they may all be gone.

What is the difference between a seal and a sea lion?

Even though seals and sea lions look very much alike, it is not hard to tell these animals apart. A sea lion

In this close-up view of a young harbor seal, the tiny holes on each side of its head are the ears. (Lynn Stone)

has small ears that can easily be seen on each side of its head, while a seal does not. Seals, though, do have ears. Their ears, however, are just tiny holes on the sides of the head.

Is a porpoise the same animal as a dolphin?

No, there is a difference between a porpoise and a dolphin. One of the best ways to tell these animals apart is to look at their faces. Dolphins have a long,

The long, narrow snouts of these bottlenose dolphins clearly show as they leap out of the sea.

narrow **snout**, while porpoises have a more rounded head and face without a snout.

Many people use both names, porpoise and dolphin, to describe the large, playful animals with streamlined bodies and smiling faces that entertain us at sea aquariums. Even though these animals are sometimes called porpoises, they are really either bottle-nosed dolphins or common dolphins.

You may sometimes see the name *dolphin* used to describe a kind of fish that lives in warm ocean water around the world. This fish, of course, is not related to the air-breathing mammals we call dolphins. It just happens to have the same name.

What is a fish?

A fish is a **cold-blooded** animal that lives in water, uses gills for breathing, uses fins for swimming, and has a backbone called a vertebra. Today, more than 25,000 kinds of fish live in the world's oceans, rivers, lakes, streams, and ponds. Of these, about 17,000 are found in our oceans.

Some animals in the oceans look like fish but are not. For example, whales and porpoises have fins and a backbone and swim in the oceans of the world, but they are not fish. Fish breathe through gills. Whales and porpoises have lungs and breathe air as you and I and other mammals do.

Other animals in the oceans that are called fish, such as starfish and jellyfish, are not fish, either. For one thing, neither of these animals has a backbone.

How do fish breathe underwater?

Fish are able to breathe underwater because of special organs in their bodies called gills. While you and I live in an ocean of air, fish live in an ocean of water. Just as we need the oxygen in the air in order to breathe, fish need the oxygen in the water to survive in their world.

To understand how gills remove oxygen from water, it helps to know how your own lungs remove oxygen from the air. When you take a deep breath, fresh air fills your lungs. Once in the lungs, some of this air moves into tiny spaces where it is separated from the blood by extremely thin tissues. Here, the oxygen moves through these thin tissues and gets absorbed into the blood passing by. The blood then carries the oxygen throughout your body to help keep all the cells alive and healthy.

THE FINS OF A FISH

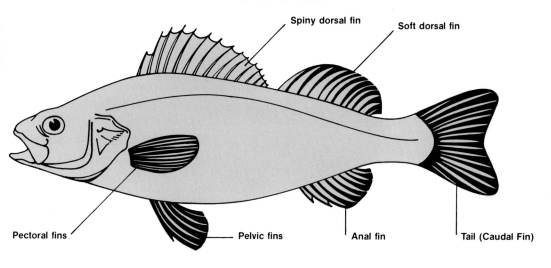

Spiny dorsal fin

Soft dorsal fin

Pectoral fins

Pelvic fins

Anal fin

Tail (Caudal Fin)

A fish has gills instead of lungs and water instead of air around it. In order to survive, a fish must keep water moving over its gills. The oxygen in the water passes through the thin tissues of the gills and gets absorbed into the blood flowing through the gills. The blood then carries the oxygen to all the living cells in the body of the fish.

Do fish, dolphins, and whales sleep?

Some, but not all, of these animals sleep. However, the way in which fish, dolphins, and whales sleep is very different from the way you and I sleep.

If you look closely at the eye of a fish, you will notice it has no eyelid. These animals, then, cannot close their eyes and must sleep with both eyes open. For fish, though, this does not seem to be a problem.

Fish have found several ways to sleep. At night, many fish simply stop swimming and remain suspended in the water between the surface and the bottom. Even though their eyes are open, these animals can rest in the darkness that surrounds them. Fish that live around a coral reef often swim into cracks and holes in the reef. There they sleep hidden from their enemies that hunt at night. Some fish sleep on the bottom, resting upright on their stomachs. Others, such as queen triggerfish, swim to the bottom and lie on their sides to sleep for the night. A fish, called a wrasse, also sleeps at the bottom on its side. However, this little animal actually covers its body with a blanket of sand. Parrotfish spend the night in an interesting way. Each night these fish secrete a thin bag of slime around their bodies. Their enemies find the slime unpleasant and leave the parrotfish alone while they sleep.

Even though many kinds of fish sleep, some do not. Examples of fish that may never sleep are tuna, flying fish, and some sharks.

Whales and dolphins are air-breathing mammals that cannot breathe underwater. If one of these animals fell into a deep sleep, as you and I do, it could sink beneath the surface and drown. Because of this danger, most dolphins and whales can take only short naps while floating just below the surface. Every few minutes the dozing animal must push its head above the water to get a breath of fresh air.

Can flying fish really fly?

Flying fish do not really fly by flapping their "wings" as a bird does. Instead, they leave the water and glide through the air just above the surface. What makes it possible for these fish to "fly" is the size and shape of their fins.

First, look at the fins on a goldfish. There is a fin on its back (dorsal fin), its tail (caudal fin), one on each of its sides (pectoral fins), one under its tail (anal fin), and two under its stomach (pelvic fins). A goldfish, however, cannot glide above the water.

The two large, winglike fins of a flying fish help it glide through the air.

Now look at the fins on a California flying fish. It, too, has the same kinds of fins as a goldfish, but the fins on the flying fish are shaped differently. The two large winglike pectoral fins, for example, are much broader than those of the goldfish. In addition, the pelvic fins on a flying fish are enlarged to help it glide through the air.

Flying fish prepare to glide above the water by swimming swiftly just below the ocean's surface. When the speed is right, the animal suddenly swims upward, passing through the ocean's surface and into the air. As the fish breaks through the surface, its winglike fins are opened, and its "flight" begins.

The distances these animals glide and the height they reach above the water depend on many things. For example, the speed with which the fish leave the water greatly affects how high and far they will go. In addition, the speed and direction of the wind can make the fish's time above the water short or long.

For many years, sailors have watched these small fish soar through the air. Some of these animals glide for distances of 164 feet (50 meters) at speeds of 35 miles per hour (56 kilometers per hour). Flying fish usually glide about 3 feet (0.9 meter) above the surface, but some get high enough to land on the decks of ships.

The fearsome large mouth and sharp teeth of a sand tiger shark stand out from the dark water in this undersea close-up view. (Jeff Rotman)

Are sharks fish?

Yes, sharks are fish. They are cold-blooded animals that live in water, use gills for breathing and fins for swimming, and have backbones called vertebrae. Any animal with all these characteristics is a fish.

Sharks, however, are quite different from most other fish. Sharks and their relatives, the rays, do not have skeletons made of bone. Instead, these animals have skeletons made of a tough, flexible material called **cartilage**.

The skin of sharks is also different from that of most fish. Even though sharks do not appear to have scales, they do. In fact, these animals have thousands of tiny, toothlike scales covering their bodies. Because of the shape of these scales, their skin feels like sandpaper.

What is the largest fish in the ocean?

The largest fish in the world is called a whale shark. This animal is a shark that may grow sixty-five to seventy feet (twenty to twenty-one meters) long and weigh more than twenty-five tons (twenty-three metric tons). No other fish reaches the size of these giants.

Despite their enormous size, whale sharks do not attack people. These fish are gentle, have very small teeth, and feed mainly on tiny plankton, sardines, and anchovies that they filter from the water as they swim through the ocean.

What kind of animal is a seahorse?

As hard as it may be to believe, a seahorse is a fish. This animal, like other fish, has fins, gills, a backbone, and lives in water. Unlike other fish, however, a sea-horse swims in a vertical, or up and down, position, instead of swimming on its stomach as most fish do.

If you look at one of these animals from the side, you can see its horselike head and neck. Because of its unusual appearance, it received the name *seahorse.*

Can a stingray really sting?

Yes, a stingray can cause a very painful wound. These flat-bodied fish have long, thin, whiplike tails equipped with a poisonous bony spine. This spine is sharp and pointed and can cut or punch a hole in a person's skin. Once the spine has opened the skin, poison from the tissue covering the spine enters the wound and causes the stinging pain.

About 100 different kinds of stingrays live in the warm, shallow ocean waters of the world. Most of these animals spend much time at the bottom or just under the sand and mud. As a result, it is very hard to see them and a person may step directly on the spine or on the resting fish. Either way, the result is usually very painful for the person wading through the water. If stepped on, the sharp, pointed spine will easily cut into the bottom of a bare foot. If, however, a person

Resting on the ocean floor in the Red Sea, the flat body and long, thin, whiplike tail of this stingray blend in with the color of the sea bottom beneath it. (Jeff Rotman)

steps on, or very near to the stingray itself, the fish can use its whiplike tail to drive the spine into the victim's leg or ankle.

If you are ever injured by a stingray, let the wound bleed to help get rid of the poison. Next, wash the injured area to prevent an infection and soak the wound in hot water for about an hour. A doctor should then check the injury because stingray wounds often become infected.

Do some fish have lights?

Yes, the bodies of some fish do have lights that can be turned on and off. The colors of these lights are often red, green, gold, orange, blue, or pink. Some fish have lights of only one color on their bodies, while others have lights of two or three different colors.

The light is produced by a special chemical known as **luciferin**. When this chemical mixes with oxygen, it glows.

The lights these animals have work in two ways. Some stay on, while others turn on and off. A flashlight fish, for example, has a large, greenish light under each eye that glows all the time. In order to keep this light from being seen, a flashlight fish covers the patch of light with a layer of skin. When the light is needed again, the patch is uncovered. But not all fish produce light that glows all the time. For example, hatchetfish and lanternfish have small light organs on the surface of their bodies. These small lights are actually turned on and off as needed.

Appendix
Scientific Names
for Sea Animals

All plants and animals have formal names and many have common names or nicknames. The formal name of a plant or animal is called the **scientific name** and it is the same all over the world. A common name, however, can be different from place to place. In addition, common names can be very confusing because different kinds of plants or different kinds of animals can have the same common name. For example, if someone said they saw a dolphin in the ocean, we cannot be sure if the dolphin was the mammal or the fish.

In the table below, you will find the common name (nickname) and the scientific name (formal name) for each plant and animal discussed in this book. Each scientific name has two parts. The first part, called the *genus*, always begins with a capital letter and is given to a small group of plants or animals that are similar to one another. The second part of the scientific name, called the *species*, is given to plants or animals that are exactly alike. For example, humans are different from all other animals. As a result, scientists give us the name *Homo* (genus) *sapiens* (species), or *Homo sapiens*.

Common Name	Scientific Name
Bull Kelp	*Nereocystis luetkeana*
Blue Whale	*Balaenoptera musculus*
Bottle-nosed Dolphin	*Tursiops truncatus*
California Flying Fish	*Cypselurus californicus*
Chicken Liver Sponge	*Chondrilla nucula*
Common Dolphin	*Delphinus delphis*
Dolphin (fish)	*Coryphaena hippurus*
Electric Catfish	*Malapterurus electricus*
Electric Eel	*Electrophorus electricus*
Electric Ray	*Torpedo nobiliana*
Elk Kelp	*Pelagophycus porra*
Fire Sponge	*Tedania ignis*
Giant Clam	*Tridacna gigas*
Giant Kelp	*Macrocystis pyrifera*
Giant Squid	*Architeuthis princeps*
Gizzard Shad	*Dorosoma cepedianum*
Irish Moss	*Chondrus crispus*
Lion's Mane	*Cyanea capillata*
Loggerhead Sponge	*Spheciospongia vesparia*
Menhaden	*Brevoortia tyrannus*
Narwhal	*Monodon monoceros*
Orange Softball Sponge	*Cinachyra kuekenthali*

Common Name	Scientific Name
Pink Jellyfish	*Cyanea capillata*
Portuguese man-of-war	*Physalia physalis*
Queen Triggerfish	*Balistes capriscus*
Rockweed	*Fucus vesiculosus*
Red Finger Sponge	*Haliclona rubens*
Sargassum	*Sargassum natans*
Sea Blubber	*Cyanea capillata*
Sea Lettuce	*Ulva lactuca*
Sea Moss	*Bryopsis plumosa*
Sea Palm	*Postelsia palmaeformls*
Sea Wasp	*Chiropsalmus quadrigatus*
Sperm Whale	*Physeter catodon*
Stinking Vase Sponge	*Ircinia campana*
Sunflower Star	*Pycnopodia helianthoides*
Whale Shark	*Rhincodon typus*
Yellow Tube Sponge	*Aplysina fistularis*

 *Glossary*

abdomen (AB-duh-muhn)—the rear section of an arthropod

antennae (an-TEHN-ee)—the sense organs or "feelers" on the heads of such animals as insects and crabs

arthropod (AHR-thruh-pahd)—a member of the large animal group—the phylum—Arthropoda (awr-THRAHP-uh-duh). These animals have legs with joints and no backbones. Insects, spiders, and crabs are arthropods

baleen (buh-LEEN)—the special material in the mouth of a toothless whale that traps plankton for the whale to eat. Baleen is made of the same tough substance that forms fingernails, claws, and horns. Baleen is sometimes called whalebone

calcium carbonate (KAL-see-uhm KAHR-buh-nayt)—a chemical compound that forms an important part of seashells, bones, and coral reefs

cartilage (KAHRT-uhl-ihj)—the tough, flexible material that forms the skeleton of sharks and rays; sometimes called gristle

chlorophyll (KLAWR-uh-fihl)—the green material in leaves and plants that uses sunlight to change carbon dioxide and water into sugar and oxygen

Cnidaria (ny-DAIR-ee-uh)—the large group, or phylum, of animals that includes jellyfish, corals, and sea anemones

cobbles—rounded rocks that are larger than pebbles but smaller than boulders. Cobbles are between 2.5 and 10 inches (6 and 25 centimeters) in diameter. These rocks are also called cobblestones

cold-blooded—an animal with a body temperature that is about the same as the air or water in which it lives. Fish and reptiles are examples of cold-blooded animals

condense—to change from a gas to a liquid

cove—a small bay or inlet with a narrow opening to a larger body of water

depression—used here to mean the huge low area in the earth's surface that holds water in the world's ocean

diatom (DY-uh-tahm)—a tiny, one-celled algae that may be green in color but is usually golden brown. Diatoms can be round, oval, rectangular, and triangular in shape. These plants are the most abundant kinds of phytoplankton in the ocean

echinoderm (ih-KY-nuh-durm)—a member of the large animal group, or phylum, Echinodermata (ee-kyn-oh-DURM-uh-tuh). This name means "spiny skin" and is used to describe a group of ocean animals that include sea urchins, sand dollars, and sea stars (starfish)

extinct (ek-STINKT)—no longer living anywhere on earth. For example, dinosaurs are extinct

flagellum (fluh-JEHL-uhm)—a long, slender thread found on certain kinds of cells. In sponges, the flagellum whips moving water through the animal's body

foraminiferan (fuh-RAM-uh-NIHF-ur-uhn)—a one-celled animal that secretes, or releases, a tiny coil-shaped shell around its soft body

guyot (GEE-oh)—a flat-topped mountain rising from the ocean floor; also called a tablemount

latitude (LAT-uh-tood)—the lines on a map or globe that circle the earth parallel to the equator. These lines are measured in degrees north and south of the equator

lava—molten rock that flows from a volcano vent during an eruption

luciferin (loo-SIHF-uh-ruhn)—a chemical found in the light-producing organs of animals such as fireflies and certain fish. When mixed with oxygen, luciferin glows

macroscopic (mak-ruh-SCOP-ik)—something that can be seen without the use of a microscope or hand lens; visible to the naked eye

mainland—a continent or large piece of land

microscope—an instrument that magnifies objects that are too small to be seen clearly with the naked eye

microscopic (my-kro-SCOP-ik)—extremely small in size; an object that can be seen only with a microscope

mineral (MIHN-ur-uhl)—a substance that is not a plant or an animal. A mineral, therefore, is not living, and never has been living. Salt, sand, stone, gold, and diamonds are minerals

mollusk (MAHL-uhsk)—an animal with no backbone and a soft body, which is usually surrounded by a hard shell. Clams and snails are examples of mollusks

offshore—in a direction away from the shore and into the ocean

phylum (FY-luhm)—a large group of plants or animals; one of the primary divisions of the plant and animal kingdoms

phytoplankton (fyt-oh-PLANK-tuhn)—the tiny plants that float near the surface of the ocean and become the food of many sea animals

polyp (PAHL-uhp)—an animal with a soft, tube-shaped body. The base of the animal is attached to the ocean bottom, while at the other end, there is a mouth surrounded by tentacles.

Porifera (poh-RIHF-ur-uh)—the large group, or phylum, of animals known as the sponges

radiolarian (ray-dee-oh-LAIR-ee-uhn)—a one-celled animal that secretes, or gives off, a round, ball-shaped shell around its soft body

ridge—a long, narrow strip of raised land

scientific name—the two part Latin name given to every different kind of *species* of plant and animal. For example, the scientific name for humans is *Homo sapiens*. Every species has its own scientific name so that a plant or animal with several common names can still be properly identified.

secrete (sih-KREET)—to form and release a substance

sediment (SED-uh-muhnt)—solid materials, such as sand, mud, and gravel, that settle to the bottom in a body of water

shingle—small, often flat stones found along the seashore

snout—the nose and jaws that stick out from the face of an animal; muzzle

tentacle (TEHN-tuh-kuhl)—a long, thin, armlike extension on a sea animal's body, used for moving, feeling, or grasping; corals and jellyfish have tentacles around their mouths

warm-blooded—an animal that has a constant, unchanging body temperature. Mammals are warm-blooded animals

waterway—a body of water that is deep enough and wide enough for boats and ships to use

weathering—the breaking down of rock and sediment at the earth's surface by water, wind, ice, and the activity of plants and animals

zooplankton (zoh-uh-PLANK-tuhn)—tiny animals that feed on phytoplankton floating in the ocean

 *Selected Bibliography*

Berger, Melvin. *Oceanography Lab.* New York: John Day, 1973.

Carson, Rachel L. *The Sea Around Us.* New York: John Day, 1973.

Challand, Helen J. *Activities in the Earth Sciences.* Chicago: Childrens Press, 1982.

Cousteau, Jacques-Yves, and Cousteau, Phillippe. *The Shark: Splendid Savage of the Sea.* New York: Doubleday, 1970.

Cousteau, Jacques-Yves, and Diole, Phillippe. *Diving Companions: Sea Lion, Elephant Seal, Walrus.* New York: Doubleday, 1974.

——. *Dolphins.* New York: Doubleday, 1974.

——. *Life and Death in a Coral Sea.* New York: Doubleday, 1971.

——. *Octopus and Squid: The Soft Intelligence.* New York: Doubleday, 1973.

——. *The Whale: Mighty Monarch of the Sea.* New York: Doubleday, 1972.

Gardner, Robert. *The Whale Watchers' Guide.* New York: Julian Messner, 1984.

Graves, Eleanor, ed. *Life in the Coral Reef.* New York: Time-Life Films, 1977.

___ . *Whales and Other Sea Mammals.* New York: Time-Life Films, 1977.

Jacobs, Francine. *An Ocean Desert: The Sargasso Sea.* New York: William Morrow, 1975.

___ . *Nature's Light: The Story of Bioluminescence.* New York: William Morrow, 1974.

Jacobson, Morris K., and Emerson, William K. *Wonders of Starfish.* New York: Dodd, Mead, 1977.

Jacobson, Morris K., and Franz, David R. *Wonders of Jellyfish.* New York: Dodd, Mead, 1978.

Kiefer, Irene. *Global Jigsaw Puzzle: The Story of Continental Drift.* New York: Atheneum, 1978.

Lambert, David. *The Ocean.* New York: Bookwright Press, 1984.

Leatherwood, Stephen, and Reeves, Randall R. *The Sierra Club Handbook of Whales and Dolphins.* San Francisco: Sierra Club Books, 1983.

Polking, Kirk. *Oceans of the World: Our Essential Resources.* New York: Philomel Books, 1983.

Poynter, Margaret. *Volcanoes, The Fiery Mountains.* New York: Julian Messner, 1980.

Settle, Mary Lee. *Water World*. New York: Lodestar Books, 1984.

Simon, Seymour. *Science at Work: Projects in Oceanography*. New York: Franklin Watts, 1972.

Waters, John F. *The Continental Shelves*. New York: Abelard-Schuman, 1975.

Zim, Herbert S. *Corals*. New York: William Morrow, 1966.

Zim, Herbert S., and Krantz, Lucretia. *Sea Stars and Their Kin*. New York: William Morrow, 1976.

Books for Younger Readers

Angel, Heather. *Life on the Seashore*. Morristown, New Jersey: Silver Burdett, 1976.

Arnold, Caroline. *Bodies of Water: Fun, Facts, and Activities*. New York: Franklin Watts, 1985.

Berger, Melvin. *Jigsaw Continents*. New York: Coward, McCann, and Geoghegan, 1977.

McClung, Robert M. *Sea Star*. New York: William Morrow, 1975.

Oxford Scientific Films. *Jellyfish and Other Sea Creatures*. New York: G. P. Putnam's Sons, 1982.

Ronai, Lili. *Corals*. New York: Thomas Y. Crowell, 1976.

Index

 ## *About the Author*

W. Wright Robinson holds a master's degree in biology and is a former instructor of biological oceanography as well as a biological researcher. His keen interest in oceanography and the high value he places on communicating his love and knowledge of the ocean to children led Mr. Robinson to write *Incredible Facts about the Ocean.*

Explaining his approach, the author states, "By using a question and answer format, each topic is explained in a way that allows the information to build gradually through a logical progression of questions. In this way, the student is guided through complex principles, learning not only the answers to questions, but also what questions to ask." The end result is a full understanding of the topic.

Mr. Robinson is currently the chairperson of the science department at King and Queen Central High School in King and Queen, Virginia. He lives in Urbanna, Virginia.